CW00350952

A Divine Gift

The Consecrated Life

by
Sr Mary David Totah, OSB

*All booklets are published thanks to the
generous support of the members of the
Catholic Truth Society*

CATHOLIC TRUTH SOCIETY
PUBLISHERS TO THE HOLY SEE

Contents

All rights reserved. First published 2014 by The Incorporated Catholic Truth Society, 40-46 Harleyford Road London SE11 5AY Tel: 020 7640 0042 Fax: 020 7640 0046. © 2014 The Incorporated Catholic Truth Society.

ISBN 978 1 78469 008 3

"A girl of eighteen named Clare, belonging to one of the noble families of Assisi, went secretly to see Br Francis and asked him to help her to live 'after the manner of the Holy Gospel.' Talking with him strengthened her desire to leave all worldly things behind and live for Christ. A few days later, she slipped away from her home and hurried through the woods to the chapel of the Portiuncula, where Francis was then living with his small community. He and his brethren had been at prayers before the altar and met her at the door with lighted tapers in their hands.

"Now about that incident I will here only say this. If it had really been a romantic elopement and the girl had become a bride instead of a nun, practically the whole modern world would have made her a heroine...modern romanticism entirely encourages such defiance of parents when it is done in the name of romantic love. For it knows that romantic love is a reality, but it does not know that divine love is a reality."

(G.K. Chesterton, *St Francis*)

A Divine Gift

"Vocation" is one of the fundamental notions of Scripture and Christian tradition. Scripture has two related concepts of vocation. There is the "absolute" vocation, the divine call to all to enter into communion with Jesus Christ. From this universal vocation, and in the service of it, flow vocations involving a "calling out": an individual or a group is chosen from among others, distinguished, given a special mission and destiny, for the sake of the rest. We may think here of Abraham, Moses and the people of Israel itself in relation to the rest of the world, and of the way Jesus called a smaller group "to be always with Him" (see *Mk* 3:1). Moreover, it was not their choice to follow Jesus, it was his choice. No one can bestow this privilege on himself, as Jesus said: "You have not chosen Me, but I have chosen you" (*Jn* 15:16).

Baptism is the consecration of those called to the Church. This universal baptismal vocation is primarily a call to holiness. Because the Church is "unfailingly holy...all in the Church are called to holiness" (*LG* 39). However, this "common vocation" to personal holiness does not abolish differences in the Church. All are called to sanctity, but "not everyone marches along the same path" (*LG* 32). There is "a wonderful diversity" in the Church of natural and supernatural gifts, of graces and charisms. This variety of gifts corresponds to a variety of states of life. The consecrated life is distinguished by being a freely given participation in the very form of life Jesus chose for himself on entering the world. "In his earthly life", he called some of his disciples "to share his experience as the chaste poor and obedient One" (*VC* 14,18), to share his own "form of life". He gave this form of life to the Church, where, thanks to the Spirit, it lives on. It is therefore a call to enter intimately into Christ's identity and mission - in St Paul's words, "to have the mind that was in Christ Jesus". "His way of living in chastity, poverty and obedience appears as the most radical way of living the Gospel on this earth, a way which may be called divine, for it was embraced by him, God and man, as the expression of his relationship as the Only-Begotten Son with the Father and with the Holy Spirit" (*VC* 18).

The call

Consecrated life is undertaken in response to a divine call (*PC* 1,5), under the influence of the Holy Spirit (*LG* 39). Even before being a response on the part of men and women who desire to follow Christ more closely, the consecrated life is a gift which comes from on high, an initiative of the Father "who draws his creatures to himself with a special love and a special mission" (VC 17). The Church teaches: "The gift of religious vocation is rooted in the gift of baptism but is 'not given to all the baptised'. It is freely given and unmerited; offered by God to those whom He chooses freely from among his people and 'for the sake of his people'."[1]

Religious life is a gift: a gift of God, a gift that has its source in God; a gift of the one who is consecrated, who joins himself to Christ by the gift of his whole life; a gift from the Church and to the Church. It is a personal gift, but one, as we shall see, that is ecclesial in scope and character. The life of consecrated chastity, poverty and obedience is a "divine gift" for the Church (LG 43), granted so that the Church may be adorned by the gifts of her children (PC 1). It is a charism in the strict biblical sense of the word: a gift bestowed on some of the faithful for the sake of the whole Church and the holiness of God's people.[2]

> "What can be sweeter to us, beloved brethren, than this voice of the Lord inviting us? Behold, in His loving kindness the Lord points out to us the way of life."
>
> (Rule of St Benedict)

Evangelical Origins of Consecrated Life

Reflecting the beauty of Christ

"His perfect offering confers an aspect of consecration upon all the events of his earthly existence." (*VC* 22)

The meaning and value of the consecrated life does not derive only from the call addressed by our Lord in view of a life entirely given to the kingdom. It results more profoundly still from the intention of Christ to communicate his own consecration, with the holiness that implies, to those who follow him. The foremost example of consecration is Jesus Christ himself. He is the Christ, the "Anointed One", meaning he belongs totally to God. He is, in his very essence, consecrated, anointed by God with the Holy Spirit.

This personal consecration of Jesus to the Father begins at the incarnation itself. In the course of his public life, Jesus defined himself as the one "whom the Father has consecrated and sent into the world" (*Jn* 10:36). The sending of the Son into the world by the Father was an act of consecration by the Father.

The incarnation is a consecration by which the power of divine love takes hold of a human life. In response to the objective consecration of his being which occurred in his humanity at the moment of the incarnation, he accepts the mission for the salvation of the world (*Jn* 17:19). He consecrates himself, by a free act of his person (intelligence, will, affection). This is what we call his subjective consecration.

We see this exceptional sacredness throughout Christ's life: the manner of his conception by the Holy Spirit (*Lk* 1:26-38), his presentation in the temple, and his baptism in the Spirit which inaugurated his ministry (*Mt* 3:13-17, *Mk* 1:9-11, *Lk* 3:21-22). The public affirmation of the Father who presents his Son to the world points to the essentially filial nature of consecration and of mission. In Jesus, consecration signifies not only the belonging of human nature to the divine, but also a basic act of homage to the Father and openness to the action of the Holy Spirit. Consecration is inseparable from the Trinitarian mystery.

Jesus's consecration culminates in his redeeming sacrifice. In the priestly prayer, Jesus declares: "... for their sake, I consecrate myself so that they too may be consecrated in truth" (*Jn* 17:19). He lives this consecration fully by consecrating himself through sacrifice, a sacrifice which reaches its intensity on the cross: "Father, into your hands I commend my spirit"

(*Lk* 23:46). There is a sacrificial aspect to consecration; consecration means both giving to God and sacrifice.

Thanks to this consecration consummated in sacrifice, the disciples will be consecrated "in truth". They will become able to receive a consecration inscribed in the profound depths of the person. Working from within the Lord's consecration, as it were, they will be collaborators of the truth, who reveal, together with him, the love of the Father; as witnesses they prolong his own consecration and manifest the generosity of the divine gift to humanity.

The consecration of Jesus, the first of God's religious, his total self-gift to the Father, was expressed in his life of chastity, poverty and obedience. These became known as the "evangelical counsels", which are based on his life and teaching as found in the Gospels. His total self-donation is defined by the evangelical counsels, even as they are the means of our salvation. His chastity, poverty and obedience were not a mere moral instruction addressed to us, but something he himself does and is. The life of the counsels is a manifestation of the heart of God.

"Solemn Profession is a holocaust, a total gift of oneself to God, and the most perfect imitation of Christ. On the day of the purification in the Temple, Jesus offered Himself to His Father without reserve; and from the time of this official oblation, so to speak, every moment of His life He did 'what pleased the Father' until on

the Cross, He pronounced His 'Consummatum Est'...
I have made a firm resolution to imitate this perfect
oblation of Jesus by transforming my profession into
a holocaust of faith, hope and charity."

(Blessed Columba Marmion, OSB
on his profession day)

Mary, model of consecration and consecrated life

"[The evangelical counsels] are able to more fully
mould the Christian man to that type of chaste and
detached life, which Christ the Lord chose for Himself
and which His Mother also embraced." (*LG* 46)

Of all those called by God to share in his holiness, to be
consecrated to him through Jesus Christ in the power
of the Spirit, no one responds more fully than Mary, the
mother of the consecrated one.

The close relationship between Mary and the
consecrated life has always been a conviction of the
Church. The Church's tradition sees her consecrated to
God in the temple at a very young age. When she was
received at the temple, Our Lady entered the service
of God. Many Church Fathers, such as St Athanasius,
St Ambrose, St Augustine and St Jerome, believed that
she had taken a vow of virginity to express her exclusive
devotion to God. This led many medieval authors to call
Mary the foundress of the consecrated life.

In order to prepare Mary for her role, after her Son, as prototype of all consecration, God consecrated her in advance, from the first moments of her existence in the immaculate conception, to the assumption, which unveiled and consummated her perfect union with God. We may also think of her as the foundation of the consecration of Christ for she gave him the humanity which allowed him to be king and priest and victim of the redemptive sacrifice. She is also the prototype of the consecration of the Church and of each Christian. She is the model of a life entirely consecrated to God, at every instant and in every dimension of her being.

Christ shares with Mary his total consecration to the Father, so that she too may make - in him and through him - a total, loving consecration of herself to God: "Behold the handmaid of the Lord, let it be done unto me according to thy word" (*Lk* 1:38). Her fidelity to her Son accompanies him even to the cross, where she stands as the Church - the consecrated people of God - one with Jesus in his consecration to the Father.

"As the sublime model of consecration to the Father, union with the Son and openness to the Spirit, ...Mary in fact is the sublime example of perfect consecration, since she belongs completely to God and is totally devoted to him. Chosen by the Lord, who wished to accomplish in her the mystery of the Incarnation, she reminds consecrated persons of the primacy of God's initiative." (*VC* 28)

As Our Lady shows, the primary subject of the consecration is God; God consecrates the person who commits himself to such a way of life, lays his hand on him. In its fundamental meaning, consecration is divinisation, the taking possession of someone or something by God himself, in view of their transformation. However, consecration also includes a response to his call, the solemn and special act by which a person assents to this act of consecration. The religious, like Our Lady, hands over the whole of his life to the service of God; he is at the service of God's plan by that gift of self. Christ and his Mother show us the beauty and the great worth of a life totally consecrated to God. Their entire earthly life was nothing but a constant "yes" to the Father.

Life According to the Evangelical Counsels

"The Church's holiness is fostered in a special way by the manifold counsels which the Lord proposes to his disciples in the Gospel for them to observe." (*LG* 42)

"The evangelical counsels of chastity dedicated to God, of poverty and obedience have their foundation in the teaching and example of the Lord. The Apostles and Fathers of the Church recommend them, and so do her doctors and pastors. They therefore constitute a gift of God which the Church has received from her Lord and which by his grace she always safeguards." (*LG* 43)

Counsels and commandments

The consecrated life is a life lived according to the evangelical counsels. They are called "evangelical" because they are based on the teaching and example of Christ as shown us in the four Gospels. What are counsels?

All are called, on the basis of the gift of the Holy Spirit received in baptism, to holiness, to the perfection of charity: love of God above all things and of neighbour as self.

In order to show us the concrete demands of charity, God has given us *commandments*, in addition to the twofold commandment of love. These are found principally in the Ten Commandments. These commandments prescribe what is of obligation. They describe the basic, indispensable requirements of love, "the first necessary step on the journey towards freedom, its starting-point" (*VS* 13). This explains the fact that they are often formulated negatively: "Thou shalt not…" For Origen, fulfilling a commandment is simply the paying off of the debt we have incurred by being implicated in Adam's sin.[3] For St Augustine, "a precept is something which it is a sin to disobey."[4] For St Thomas, "a precept imports necessity…the precepts of the New Law are understood to have been given with reference to those things which are necessary for attaining the end of eternal beatitude."[5]

Besides its precepts or commandments, the New Law also includes the evangelical *counsels*.

Commandments *oblige* everyone, under pain of sin, to those essential things without which charity would not exist. Counsels *invite*, not under pain of sin, and in a way adapted to each one's vocation, to those better things by which charity is developed. For Origen, therefore, virginity or voluntary almsgiving is "offered as something beyond what is owed." For St Augustine, whereas to violate a commandment is sin, to refuse to follow a counsel is not, but simply the choosing of a lesser good. Conversely, to take up a counsel is to do something "better" and "worthy of praise". For St Thomas, counsels are appropriate to the New Law, which is a law of freedom; they are something freely chosen. They "concern those things by which a man can gain the aforesaid end [eternal beatitude] better and more expeditiously." For St Francis de Sales, counsels are invitations springing from the friendliness of Christ. Lumen Gentium uses the phrase "beyond the measure of the commandment".

> "The commandments were given to all Christians and it is understood that every Christian observes them; this is, as it were, the tribute appointed to be paid to the King. Anyone who says, 'I will not pay tribute,' will he escape punishment? There are, however, in the world great and illustrious men who not only pay the appointed tribute, but also offer gifts... So also the holy Fathers not only kept the commandments but also offered gifts to God. These gifts are virginity and poverty. These are not commanded but freely given. Nowhere is it written, you shall not take a wife or beget children. Neither did Christ give the commandment, 'Sell your property!'... [He said] 'If

you want to be perfect, sell your property and give the money to the poor,' etc. See, he did not say 'sell your property' as a commandment, but as a counsel. This is clear from the condition imposed, 'If you wish to be perfect.' As we said, therefore, the Fathers offered to God besides all the other virtues, their virginity and poverty as a gift."

(Dorotheus of Gaza: *On Renunciation*)

The evangelical counsels

"If you would be perfect..." (*Mt* 19:5)

L umen Gentium speaks of the "manifold counsels". "In the Gospel there are many exhortations that go beyond the measure of the commandment, indicating not only what is 'necessary' but what is 'better'. Thus for example the exhortation not to judge (see *Mt* 7:1), to lend 'expecting nothing in return' (*Lk* 6:35), to comply with all the requests and desires of our neighbour (see *Mt* 5:40-42), to invite the poor to a meal (see *Lk* 14:13-14), to pardon always (see *Mt* 6:14-15) and many other invitations" (*RD* 9). In addition to the familiar trio of chastity, poverty and obedience, St Francis de Sales mentions almsgiving and hospitality outside cases where they would be of precept, withdrawal into solitude, continual prayer and taking the initiative in making peace with an enemy.[6]

Tradition has focussed especially on the three counsels which sum up Jesus's way of life, and it is these the consecrated profess.[7] For St John Paul II, "If, in accordance with Tradition, the profession of the evangelical counsels has concentrated on the three points of chastity, poverty and obedience, this usage seems sufficiently clear to emphasise their importance as key elements and in a certain sense as a 'summing-up' of the entire economy of salvation" (*RD* 9). They are a synthesis of the demands of the gospel. For those who profess these three evangelical counsels, they are what fill and engage their lives.

We find this trio of poverty, chastity and obedience used for the first time as the object of religious profession in the constitutions of the Trinitarians from the year 1198. From then on they became the content of the vows of all later religious orders.[8] In the *Summa Theologiae* of St Thomas Aquinas, these three counsels become the basis of a theology of religious life. Both Canon Law and the Magisterium would take it up.[9] Thus it has become the common teaching of the Church that it is the profession of these three evangelical counsels which forms the essence of the consecrated or religious life.

Why these three? In the Gospels there is a quite explicit call to *poverty* in Matthew 19:16-26, which begins with the dialogue between Jesus and a wealthy young man: "If you would be perfect, go sell what you possess and give to the poor...and come, follow me" (*Mt* 19:21).

In the Gospel of Matthew (19:3-12) when Jesus re-affirms the indissolubility of marriage, and the disciples conclude, "it is not expedient to marry", Jesus responds by offering the counsel of *celibacy* "for the sake of the kingdom of heaven", as a voluntary gift. "Not all can receive this word, but those to whom it is given... He who can receive it, let him receive it." Celibacy or consecrated chastity is not proposed as a general commandment, but rather as a recommendation, an offer, an invitation. "If virginity were commanded, marriage would seem to be forbidden," said St Jerome. It presupposes a special gift or grace of the Holy Spirit. It enables those who accept it to be more closely united to God, and it is a closer imitation of Christ, himself a virgin.

The counsel of *obedience* is drawn from Jesus's own example, which sums up his life as Redeemer. In speaking of Christ's humility, St Paul said that Jesus was obedient to God his Father "unto death, even death on a cross" (*Ph* 2:8). Jesus obeyed God in all that he did. "For I have come down from heaven, not to do my will, but the will of Him who sent me" (*Jn* 6:38). All that Jesus has and is, he has received from God the Father. From all eternity, the Son has listened to the Father in order to do his work and to accomplish his will. In consequence he shows himself freely obedient to all that incarnates this will: Jewish law, his parents, authority.

Their significance and value

A path to holiness "Transforming the human heart..." (*RD* 9)

"For the counsels, willingly undertaken in accordance with the personal vocation of each individual, contribute not a little to the purification of the heart and to spiritual freedom..." (*LG* 46)

The counsels are, in the first place, an especially effective means of attaining holiness, which is one of the goals of the consecrated life.

How are the counsels a path to holiness? They cut away hindrances to the service of God. Observance of the evangelical counsels frees the human heart from attachments to worldly things, and therefore constitutes a particularly effective means of attaining that perfection of love in which Christian perfection consists.[10] For St Thomas they are helpful as a means to give ourselves to God more fully and freely, "contemplating Him, loving Him and accomplishing his will." They help us to attain to a perfect love by putting to one side everything which might impede the movement of mind and heart towards God. Freed from the competing attractions of wealth, worldly pleasures, honour and independence, the religious is immersed in God's presence, wholly available to the plan and will of the Beloved. "Our hearts," St Thomas says, "cannot reach out totally to several things at the same time." And "since man has been placed by God between the things of this world and spiritual goods wherein eternal happiness consists, the more he cleaves to the one, the more he withdraws from the other."[11]

A spiritual therapy

In the second place, the three counsels counter the "three-fold concupiscence" (*1 Jn* 2:16) that's in us as a legacy of original sin. Through the Fall, our original wholeness was lost and sexual desire, the will to ownership and moral autonomy became unbalanced and revealed their capacity to sidetrack love. Through the profession of the counsels, Christ has opened the road back - and forward - to the fullness of love, for the consecrated state both recalls man to original holiness and anticipates the life of heaven where God will be all in all.[12]

The Preface for Religious in the Roman Missal speaks of "the wonders of your providence, by which you call human nature back to its original holiness and bring it to experience on this earth the gifts you promise in the new world to come." Therefore religious life looks backward to man's original state in paradise and forward to the life of the world to come. Adam and Eve enjoyed a threefold harmony before the fall, one that corresponds to the evangelical counsels. Their mind was set on God; God's will was their rule of life. Their obedience was the instrument by which they accepted the will of God. In their chaste lives, they reflected the chaste fruitfulness of the Trinity itself; moreover they did not experience any conflict between their spiritual life and their bodily life. Finally, they had the right attitude towards the goods of creation. They possessed nothing for themselves which they did not receive from God and had no yearning to possess anything in such a way as to exclude anyone, but were content to use what was necessary for them.

As a result of original sin and the disorder set up in our tendencies, we are excessively occupied with our own person, desires, thoughts and needs. The three counsels are means, under grace, for purifying the human heart and turning it back towards God; they are at the heart of the economy of redemption, and therefore prepare for the renewal of creation and the final transformation of the world. "The profession of chastity, poverty and obedience is a warning not to underestimate the wound of original sin and, while affirming the value of created goods, it relativizes them by pointing to God as the absolute good" (*VC* 87).

In *Vita Consecrata* 87-91, the three counsels are seen as a "spiritual therapy", not only for those who profess them, but for the world and the Church as a whole. They are a prophetic counter-statement to the three great contemporary challenges: first, that of "a hedonistic culture" which "idolizes the sexual instinct", to which "the reply of the consecrated life is above all in the joyful living of perfect chastity" (*VC* 88); second, "that of a materialism which craves possessions, heedless of the needs and sufferings of the weakest, and lacking any concern for the balance of natural resources", to which "the reply of the consecrated life is found in the profession of evangelical poverty" (*VC* 89); third, that which "comes from those notions of freedom which separate this fundamental human good from its essential relationship to the truth and to moral norms", to which "[a]n effective response ...is the obedience which marks the consecrated life" (*VC* 91).

The language of love

Thirdly, the counsels "keep ablaze continually the fervour of charity" (*LG* 46).

As we have seen, the counsels are a means towards the re-establishment of perfect love in the human heart. Here, the perspective is opposite: the counsels are expressions of a real love already present. There is, of course, no real contradiction. The vowed life is a consecration, or setting aside, of something good and precious, to offer it as a pleasing gift to one whom we love. It is an act of offering of the best things that we have.

Love naturally tends to "hand the lover over" to the beloved. Taken together, consecrated chastity, poverty and obedience make this possible; they articulate this total gift; they are the language of love.

Since the 12th century, the three counsels/vows have been understood as embracing the *totality* of life - all the (external) goods of this world that one has at one's disposal; all one's corporal goods, i.e. one's body; and all one's spiritual goods, namely, memory, understanding and will. Thus the profession of the counsels is also an expression of love, of the desire to give oneself. For this love, everything is renounced or better handed over to the Lord for his purposes. This can be linked with St Thomas's understanding of profession as a "holocaust", a perfect sacrifice.[13] The vows are not so much a series of obligations as a total dedication of one's life. *Lumen Gentium* says that in profession religious give themselves "completely to God who is loved above all" (44); they have "handed over their entire lives to his service" (*PC* 5).

The imitation of Christ

Finally, the counsels "are able to bring the Christian into a greater conformity with that kind of virginal and poor life which Christ the Lord chose for himself and which his virgin mother embraced" (*LG* 46). The counsels make possible "a Christi-form life". As *Vita Consecrata* expressed it: "By the profession of the evangelical counsels the characteristic features of Jesus - the chaste, poor and obedient One - are made constantly 'visible' in the midst of the world" (*VC* 1).

The starting point here is Christ himself and the fact that he, the Son of God, lived a "chaste, poor and obedient life." It is by looking at consecrated chastity, poverty and obedience in Christ that we shall best perceive their meaning and value. In the Trinitarian perspective adopted by *Vita Consecrata*, this way in which the Incarnate Word chose to live his life brings into the world the "ways" of the Trinity; it reflects his eternal relationship, in the Spirit, with the Father. Chastity, therefore, "is a reflection of the infinite love which links the three divine Persons." Poverty is "an expression of that total gift of self which the three divine Persons make to one another." Obedience "is a reflection in history of the loving harmony between the three divine Persons" (*VC* 21). He lived these out most fully in the gift of himself on the cross.

Life according to the counsels, therefore, "has the duty of making somehow present the way of life which Jesus himself chose" (*VC* 29); it is a "conforming of one's whole existence to Christ in an all-encompassing commitment which foreshadows the eschatological perfection", a "profound 'configuration' to the mystery of Christ" (*VC* 16). As "the prolongation in history of a special presence of the Risen Lord" (*VC* 19), the consecrated life is "a living tradition of the Saviour's life and message" (*VC* 22). And the culminating appeal to those who profess the counsels can only be: "Do not forget that you, in a very special way, can and must say that you not only belong to Christ but that 'you have become Christ'!" (*VC* 109).

Consecrated chastity

In the past the preferred order of their naming was "poverty, chastity and obedience." In Vatican II and subsequently, the order of the first two has been inverted, chastity thus coming first. Chastity is given priority because, historically, it was the first, most visibly lived counsel. The vow of consecrated chastity is the "original vow", the New Testament vow. Long before organised religious life came into being, men and women embraced the vow of celibacy to give themselves entirely to our Lord and his service. Theologically, it is given priority because of its dignity (see *LG* 42), and because the profession of it alone is enough to constitute someone as consecrated. In *Vita Consecrata*, one of the richest and most important recent papal documents on consecrated life, it is called "the first and essential" evangelical counsel (*VC* 16); in *VC* 32, "the 'door' of the whole consecrated life". As John Paul II explained, "The Council...expressly mentions consecrated chastity before the other two vows (see *LG* 43; *PC* 12,13,14), because it considers chastity as the determining commitment of the state of consecrated life. It is also the evangelical counsel that most obviously shows the power of grace" (General Audience, 16 November 1994).

In the gospel, Christ teaches that there are those who live chaste, unmarried lives for the sake of the kingdom (see *Mt* 19:10-12). Some make themselves "incapable" of marriage, in consequence of something that has happened to them, namely the kingdom. When Jesus taught people to pray for the coming of the kingdom as something future, he also wanted them to recognise the gift as already present and offered in himself. Instead of saying "for the sake of the kingdom", he could equally well have said, "because of me". From the very beginning of the Church's life, there are those who have recognised this and followed him. They renounced marriage because the sheer joy of finding the kingdom possesses them and fills their horizon. The kingdom is not first and foremost a demand for self-sacrifice, but an overwhelming gift of God, something coming with Christ.

Consecrated virginity demands a gift of self so complete that there is no room for any other union, however good in itself. So consecrated chastity is much more than an unmarried state. It is about loving Christ for himself and in himself without an intermediary. Consecrated members of the Church profess celibacy in order to belong exclusively to Christ.

Bridal union

St John Paul II sums up the teaching of the Church when he explains that, whereas marriage introduces the spouses into the mystery of Christ's union with his Church, "the profession of virginity or celibacy enables consecrated persons to share more directly in the mystery of this marriage. While conjugal love goes to Christ the bridegroom through a human union, virginal love goes directly to the person of Christ through an immediate union with Him, without intermediaries - a truly complete and decisive spiritual espousal. Thus in the person of those who profess and live consecrated chastity, the Church expresses her union as bride with Christ the bridegroom to the greatest extent. For this reason it must be said that the virginal life is found at the heart of the Church" (23 November 1994).

By uniting himself to humanity in the flesh, God accomplished a union between man and himself so profound that in the face of this reality, human marriage becomes a figure. This, of course, in no way contradicts the beauty and grandeur of marriage. Indeed, St Paul tells us that love of husband and wife is an image of the love of Christ and his Church. Earthly marriage, he teaches, is not just earthly; it is partially heavenly, since the husband is to look upon his wife not just as a woman, but as Christ looks upon the Church. And the woman is to look upon her husband not just as a man, but as Christ. What married persons do through intermediaries, consecrated persons do directly, and in that way show that their state of life already celebrates that marriage which is not temporary or passing, but which is eternal. The human love which the sacrament sanctifies is the image of the reality and not the reality itself. Consecrated chastity points to the reality of which marriage offers an image and a partial realisation: the union of Christ and the Church, of the Word of God and humanity.

In 1 Corinthians 7, St Paul discusses various issues concerning marriage and celibacy. In verses 25-38, while making it clear that he does not forbid marriage, that marriage is good, he gives it as his *counsel* that to remain celibate - as he himself is (v.7) - is "better", since it allows for an undivided, undistracted concern with the Lord. St Paul regards this as a "gift from God".

This spousal dimension is part of all consecrated life. When a saint evokes his relationship of love with the Lord, he speaks spontaneously of himself in the feminine. St Bernard speaks of the soul as the Bride of the Word, just as St John of the Cross and Blessed Charles de Foucauld look upon Christ as 'husband of their souls', and speak of 'Jesus the Bridegroom'.

Consecrated members of the Church profess celibacy or virginity in order to belong exclusively to Christ. This certainly means physical chastity; but this physical chastity is fruitful for the Church when it has its foundation in the love of God and neighbour. Chastity, then, involves not only the body, but the mind, heart and will as well. All our powers of loving are increased by this total consecration. To vow celibacy for the kingdom is to affirm by one's whole life the unique way in which God loves and is loved. It is a love affair, with God and others, and love alone can bring out the full meaning of celibacy. Those who renounce married life for the sake of the kingdom are called to become spiritual mothers and fathers in the Church. They give their lives so that Christ can be born in the hearts of many and that he can grow in the hearts and souls of others. It is not a question of loving less but of loving more, it is intensification, a magnification of love. It is a call to high love and spiritual fruitfulness.

"Behold, what I longed for, I now see; what I hoped for, I now possess; I am united in heaven to Him whom on earth I have loved with all my heart." (St Agnes)

"To love chastity... To prefer nothing to the love of Christ." (*Rule of St Benedict*)

"Thoughts on St Luke's Day after my vows: Unto the Crucified my soul is spouse, and she must likewise be, even with his body, crucified. For likeness is the cause of love, unlikeness of disunity."

(Blessed Robert Southwell, SJ, 1561-1595)

Poverty

"Even before being a service on behalf of the poor, evangelical poverty is a value in itself, since it recalls the first of the beatitudes in imitation of the poor Christ. Its primary meaning in fact is to attest that God is the true wealth of the human heart." (*VC* 90)

Consecrated men and women renounce things that are not necessary in order to receive the riches of the faith, the riches of God. With these treasures from above they are able to enrich the lives of many, in imitation of Christ himself who "though He was rich, yet for your sake became poor, so that by His poverty you might become rich" (*2 Co* 8:9). We are poor for God is everything to us. "Poverty proclaims that God is man's only real treasure... [It is] an expression of that total gift of self" (*VC* 21). Poverty is thus something close to obedience and celibacy.

The demand of Jesus is twofold: to be poor, and to the chosen disciples, to leave everything. For the latter, perfect poverty is one with perfect following and perfect obedience: at the call of Christ, they must leave everything (*Lk* 5:11,28), renounce all that they have (*Lk* 14:33) and distribute it to the poor, without taking farewells. This unconditional *leaving* of all things is the presupposition for the *readiness* for all things on the part of the disciple: not only a general readiness, with loins girt for the approaching kingdom of God, but the readiness here and now to let oneself be at the service of the kingdom without pay, without means of support, and even spiritually poor, because the Spirit will inspire what is needed.

The evangelical counsel of poverty involves not simply the possession or non-possession of material goods, but much more fundamentally, the attitude we have towards all possessions, towards created things. It means being content with what we have, and being attached to nothing, in both material and spiritual goods. The consecrated person restricts his necessities, he learns to live with less, he grows in his desire to sacrifice, he wants to have less. His wealth is God himself. The vow of poverty also means using what we have - material goods, talents, time, education, etc. - for the building up of the kingdom of God, and recognising that all that we have comes from God. As St Paul asked: "What have you that you did not receive?" (*1 Co* 4:7). The foundation of evangelical poverty is a sincere and fervent gratitude for everything. This poverty does not mean wearing rags, nor does it mean living in luxury. It is never only material, nor is it ever simply spiritual or theoretical. It is an interior disposition of detachment from things and from oneself. This poverty makes the consecrated person truly free and joyful.

"And St Francis added: 'My dear and beloved Brother, the treasure of blessed poverty is so very precious and divine that we are not worthy to possess it in our bodies. For poverty is that heavenly virtue by which all earthly and transitory things are trodden under foot, and by which every obstacle is removed from the soul so that it may freely enter into union with the eternal Lord God. It is also the virtue which makes the soul, while still here on earth, converse with the angels in Heaven. It is she who accompanied Christ on the Cross, was buried with Christ in the Tomb, and with Christ was raised and ascended into Heaven, for even in this life she gives to souls who love her the ability to fly to Heaven, and she alone guards the armour of true humility and charity.'"

(*The Little Flowers of St Francis of Assisi*)

Obedience

"To do your will, O my God" (*Ps* 40(39))

St Thomas Aquinas argues that obedience is "the principle one among the vows of religion".[14] His reasoning is that it offers to God what is most precious and central to the human person, his own will, and therefore best fulfils the purpose of the religious life. He also maintains that the other vows are included under obedience. Note the theocentric character of obedience; it is an offering to God. Obedience is at the very root of our religious life because in this vow we give not only a part of ourselves; it is our whole being that we give, since our wills dispose all our activity and moral life.

The word "to obey" comes from *ob-audire*, to listen, to listen carefully, to pay attention: "My people would not listen to me; Israel would not obey me" (*Ps* 80). The beginning of true obedience is to hearken to another and respond. It is an antecedent state of openness, a willingness to listen combined with the recognition that this responsiveness may involve changing one's life in accordance with what one hears.

As with the other two evangelical counsels, obedience is not something we do; it is first and fundamentally an attitude. For consecrated men and women, obedience does not begin with the Superior. It begins with God. We follow Christ who was himself obedient to the Father unto death. Obedience is the thread which runs throughout the whole life of our Lord: from the incarnation in Mary to his death for us on the cross, the Son obeys the Father. All his work is marked by obedience, by the readiness to let himself be disposed of by the Father according to his total will. "My food is to do the will of the Father" (*Jn* 4:34); "I always do what pleases Him" (*Jn* 8:29). Obedience allows us to belong totally to God. It makes us see God as the source of the unfolding of our lives. Our obedience to God's commandments and discipline is the exclusive sign of our love for him and his Son.

This obedience is then furthered and made manifest in the obedience to a Superior, who discerns the will of God with and for a person. This obedience is best understood not merely as an external performance, but in terms of faith, hope and love. We are asked to exercise our faith to believe that what comes to us through obedience is what God wants of us here and now; it is faith since we express our belief in the will of God who conceals himself in the person of our Superior. Obedience implies hope as well - that what we are doing will somehow co-operate with God's purposes.

Love and freedom

By our obedience we show not only our faith and hope but also our love, because obedience unites our will to God, to the Beloved which is the basis of love. The one who obeys shows himself to be in tune, in agreement with the will of God. And through this obedience in faith we are being guided into the service of our neighbour in Christ. Obedience is love in action; when one loves, one eagerly grasps and affirms the desires of the one whom one loves. The essence of obedience is to put God and others before oneself. Our obedience is not only the expression of faith in God and love for God; it is also the expression of love of others. Obedience in faith is ordered to the service of others, to fraternal charity, to the service of the whole Church. Obedience in faith and love, then, shows that to give up one's own will does not mean not to have a will, but to harness one's will to one's faith and one's love. As an attitude, it finds expression in all of life's situations because God speaks to us in all life's situations.

Vatican II speaks of "freedom strengthened by obedience" (*LG* 43). One becomes truly free when one finds and accepts one's identity as a child of God and expresses this relationship in obedience. Obedience is given to us to make possible a relationship of love. Freedom is not something absolute and independent that can grow and reach perfection apart from God. When we yield our freedom to God who created it, we find it.

Obedience is never a relinquishing of human responsibility for life and activity; it is a light that clarifies what the Lord wants of us here and now regarding our task in the fulfilment of the immense plan of God. It springs from the very reality of our vocation as created beings whose truth is bound up with the will of the Creator; and in the order of redemption, obedience unites us to our obedient Saviour, the sharing in his sufferings in order to follow him into his kingdom. It is the very shape of a life given to God. It is an enlightened attitude of availability and receptivity to every sign of the will of God coming to us from within or without. Like Mary's *fiat*, obedience is a profound "Yes" to life, an act of faith in the activity of God in and through life. Origen said that Mary's *fiat* was as if she were saying, "Behold I am a tablet to be written on, let the Lord of all things do with me as he wishes." This is an attitude of self-surrender which is at the same time extremely active, active because ready to respond to God's every suggestion, every call.

"The first degree of humility is obedience without delay. This obedience is characteristic of those who prefer nothing to Christ... It is of these that the Lord said: 'At the hearing of the ear they have obeyed Me.'"

(*Rule of St Benedict*)

"And though I wish you all perfection in every virtue and spiritual gift, it is true...that it is in obedience, more than in any other virtue, that God our Lord gives me the desire to see you stand out... And insofar as this virtue flourishes, all the other virtues will flourish and bring forth the fruit which I desire in your souls, and which He claims who, by His obedience, redeemed the world after it had been destroyed by the lack of it, becoming obedient unto death, even death on a cross [*Ph* 2:8]... [I]n the purity and perfection of obedience together with the true surrender of our wills and judgement, I am very desirous, my dear brothers, that they who serve God in this Society should be conspicuous, so that by this virtue its true sons may be recognized as men who regard not the person whom they obey, but in him Christ our Lord, for whose sake they obey."

(St Ignatius of Loyola, *Letter on Obedience*, 1553

The Vowed Life

"It is the *profession* of these counsels, within a permanent state of life recognized by the Church, that characterizes the life consecrated to God." (*CCC* 915)

As we have seen, the practice of the counsels, at least in spirit, belongs to the Christian life as such. Consecrated persons practise the three major counsels according to the letter also, and commit themselves to them by vow, under a rule approved by the Church. So it is not the practice of the counsels as such which characterises the consecrated life. It is rather the profession of the three "great" counsels by a lifelong vow. The charism that is the consecrated life is of a special order: it is ordained not towards some particular actions or tasks for the Church, but towards a permanent form of life.

Vows and profession

A vow is a promise made to God. That is how the *Code of Canon Law* describes it, following the teaching of St Thomas (Can. 1191,1). The taking of a vow is firstly an action which occurs between God and the individual person: the person promises to God to do or not to do something. Its great value and peculiar character resides in the fact that it is made to God himself. This can be a private event; one then speaks of a private vow. But even when a vow is made in the presence of many witnesses, it is not *ipso facto* a public vow. A public vow requires acceptance by a legitimate superior in the name of the Church (Can. 1192,2). It is clear that religious vows are in this sense public vows (Can. 656,5) even if, as in times of persecution, they can only be made in secret or in hiding. Moreover, in religious commitment, it is not just a particular action which we promise to God (e.g. a pilgrimage); it is a dedication, something which affects the whole person.

The public character of religious profession makes clear that profession is not simply about a personal relationship with God, even if this is the basis for everything else. There is a second element involved: the *ecclesial dimension*. "By religious profession members assume by public vow the observance of the three evangelical counsels, are consecrated to God through the ministry of the Church and are incorporated into the institute by rights and duties defined by law" (Can. 654).

Thus the following elements constitute the nature of profession:

(a) It is the *making of a vow*, *a public vow*, i.e. a vow acknowledged and accepted by the Church.

(b) Profession is *an action in the Church and for the Church*. The religious is consecrated to God "through the ministry of the Church". How do we know that God has really said, "Henceforth I have laid my hand on you and accepted the gift of your life to use it as I please"? Through his Church. The vows consecrate our life and person to the service of God and to the Church.

(c) Further, *religious profession is made in a particular institute and in a particular community*. Every religious is a member of a community acknowledged by the Church. Consecration binds us to a community governed by a rule of life.

(d) Finally, religious profession constitutes a *handing over, a sacrifice of oneself to God through the three vows*. The basis of the religious commitment, its real heart, is the total dedication of oneself to God.

"There is indeed nothing more liberating than the taking of solemn vows...you give your riches to the poor and yourselves to God; you have nothing you can call your own, not even, in a sense, yourselves. You lay yourselves symbolically on the altar when your vows are put there at the Offertory. That is you. Your gifts. Everything God has given you. And the Church, who accepts this gift of yourselves in the

name of God, will direct you in the name of God...
Make your gift wholeheartedly. Make your gift
recklessly. Love is reckless."

(Cardinal Basil Hume, OSB)

The virtue of religion

The consecrated life is also sometimes called *the religious
life*.[15] This is because, as a deliberate promise made to
God, the vow comes under the virtue of religion, which
is the first of the moral virtues; this virtue "prostrates" us
before God's infinite majesty. It recognises that man is
a created being, ordered towards his Creator and Lord,
to whom he owes praise, reverence and the service of
his being. The religious life proceeds from the virtue of
religion. Religious consecration, consisting of the vow
of the counsels, ratified and accepted by the Church,
is the offering of our whole self and the recognition
of God's dominion over our whole being. It is a
complete act of adoration and the full response to our
baptismal consecration.

The effect of the vow of religion is not only to oblige
the religious to practise the evangelical counsels, but
also and especially to consecrate him entirely to God
and to his service. In other words, the effect of the vows
is not a negative one of renunciation and liberation;
they are directly and positively a worship of God. Thus
all the virtuous acts of the religious, all his good works,

are consecrated to God and become acts of worship, even the humblest ones.

St Thomas also says the profession brings about a real transfer of property; the religious no longer belongs to himself; he belongs to God as a consecrated object, as a chalice. St Thomas notes that the only way for a human being to offer his or her whole life to God all at once is to make a solemn vow which offers not only virtuous actions, but even their source, the very capability to produce them.[16] Here St Thomas refers to a story told by St Anselm: someone used to offer one of his friends the fruits of a tree in his orchard; then he thought he would do better by giving him the tree itself. Likewise, comments St Thomas, he who takes a vow does not offer God only virtuous acts, but the very root of his acts, the power to produce them, the whole tree.

> "O My Divine Redeemer, why can I not by a thousand thousand vows attach myself so closely to you that, not only will I never be separated from you, but I will become even one with you."
>
> (St Claude de la Colombiere)

Baptism and religious profession

St Thomas Aquinas saw in the act of religious profession an objective consecration of a person, analogous to, though not identical with, the sacramental consecration in episcopal ordination. Vatican II teaches the same. Religious profession is consecratory in nature.[17]

Is there a distinct consecration involved in religious profession or is it nothing other than baptismal consecration drawn out to its most perfect expression? As *Vita Consecrata* explains, the religious life is a new and special consecration, "a special and fruitful deepening of the consecration received at baptism", "the close union with Christ already begun at baptism develops into the gift of a fuller, more explicit, and authentic configuration to Him through profession of the evangelical counsels" (*VC* 30).

To clarify the difference, a distinction needs to be made between objective consecration and subjective consecration. As we have seen, the consecration of Christ is the exemplar of all Christian consecration. In his incarnation, Christ is set apart, reserved by the Father for a special mission - this is objective consecration. But Christ is also consecrated by his free acceptance of this role and his own self-offering to the Father - this is subjective consecration.

In baptism the objective consecration is received when the sacrament is conferred; but only when a person freely embraces God's gift to him is he subjectively consecrated. In the sacrament of baptism, the obstacles separating a person from the life of Christ are removed; the subjective consecration means responding to the gift.

All reborn in Christ are called to live out chastity proper to their state, obedience to God and the Church, and a reasonable detachment from material possessions. But baptism does not in and of itself include the call to celibacy or virginity, renunciation of possessions, and obedience to a superior according to a rule. These are particular gifts, not given to everyone, as emphasised by our Lord with respect to celibacy (*Mt* 19:10-12). The difference, then, is that baptism initiates a life of personal growth towards conformity to Christ, while religious consecration goes beyond that and expresses, in a person's complete commitment of a whole life, what such conformity means.

Religious profession is a consecration rooted in baptism, but which is at the same time a new intervention on the part of God. Religious life is a divine and positive intervention to which an active response is given which affects the whole person.

Unlike marriage and priestly ordination, the profession of the evangelical counsels is not a new sacrament. As a "fuller expression" of baptism (*PC* 5), "the special consecration" of religious does not give new special powers in the Church, but it actualises in an explicit manner that vocation to which all are called by virtue of their baptismal consecration. This is one reason why it is not separate sacrament.

"O Jesus, my divine spouse! May I never lose the second robe of my Baptism! Take me before I can commit the slightest voluntary fault. May I never seek nor find anything but yourself alone... Jesus, may I die a martyr for you. Give me martyrdom of heart or of body, or rather give me both...give me the grace to fulfil my vows in all their perfection, and make me understand what a real spouse of yours should be... May your will be done in me perfectly, and may I arrive at the place you have prepared for me... Jesus, allow me to save very many souls; let no soul be lost today; let all the souls in purgatory be saved... I only want to give you joy and to console you."

(St Thérèse of Lisieux on her profession day,
8 September 1890)

The Ecclesial Nature of Consecrated Life

As Vatican II explained, "the evangelical counsels unite those who practise them to the Church and her mystery in a special way" (*LG* 44). Christ calls and consecrates some to use them for the upbuilding of the Church (*Ep* 4:12).

States of life within the Church

The "common vocation" to personal holiness does not negate differences in the Church. The variety of gifts in the Church corresponds to three states of Christian life: the priesthood, the consecrated life, the lay life or marriage. Each is entrusted with the task of expressing in its own way one or other aspect of the mystery of Christ. The common denominator is the vocation of all to holiness, the vocation of all the baptised.

The mission of the ministerial priesthood is a particular form of participation in Christ's priesthood, offering authoritative mediation between God and his people. The mission of the laity to clergy and religious is to order the temporal affairs of the world according to God's plan; they represent the Church's insertion into the world. The mission of consecrated persons is to be a living sign which inspires clergy and laity to the intimate love and worship of God. The call to this intimate form of discipleship is, of course, common to all Christians, but in the case of those called to the consecrated life, it takes on an objectivity which confronts the whole Church with the priority of Christ and the demands of the gospel. The hierarchy, the consecrated life, and marriage all refer to something more than themselves. The life of consecrated persons signifies that the holiness of the gift received in the Church must culminate in the holiness of a life given in return.

Consecrated life as epiphany

"The profession of the evangelical counsels, then, appears as a sign which can and ought to attract all the members of the Church to an effective and prompt fulfilment of the duties of their Christian vocation." (*LG* 44)

This total gift of self through the three evangelical counsels is a *sign* for others, an "epiphany" in the Church, a shining forth. The consecrated life is a sign; it shows, it manifests. To signify does not mean to exclude but to indicate. To signify is to refer to the whole by a part which suggests it. What does the consecrated life "signify"?

Sign of the Church's holiness

"Christian holiness is fostered by the [evangelical] counsels" (*LG* 42)

The Church is holy, because Christ who "alone is holy... joined her to himself" as his Body and his Bride (*LG* 39). Catholic tradition makes a distinction between the holiness *of* the Church and the holiness *in* the Church, between the holiness of the Church as a supernatural reality and the holiness demanded from individual Christians. It roots the latter in the former: the holiness of the faithful is the consequence and the manifestation of the holiness of the Church. They are called to be holy, because the Church, whose members they are, is "unfailingly holy". We enter into the holiness of the Church by our baptism.

The Church has always seen in the profession of the evangelical counsels a special path to holiness. This does not mean that religious are examples of personal sanctity, but that the basic shape of the consecrated life manifests the basic shape of Christian sanctity: "Through the deeper consecration made to God it clearly shows and signifies the intimate nature of the Christian vocation" (*AG* 18). All the faithful are called to perfect sanctity, but consecrated persons do so by the profession and practice of the evangelical counsels. They are those who "tend toward holiness by a narrower path,

[and] stimulate their brethren by their example" (*LG* 13). The way of religious, and other Christians committed to the practice of the evangelical counsels, is called the "narrower path" not because it leads to a higher degree of sanctity, but because it calls for the acceptance of renunciations not demanded from all the faithful. Moreover, those in the consecrated life "*tend* towards holiness"; profession demands not sanctity acquired, but sanctity ever in process of realisation. The consecrated life implies an obligation, not of being a saint, but of striving generously to become one.

Vatican II, following St Thomas,[18] sees Christian holiness, or the "fullness of Christian life" to which all are called, as consisting in the perfection of love (*LG* 32, 40), the fulfilment of the double commandment of love: to love God with our whole heart and one another as Christ loved us.

Jesus is the primary example of perfect love. For this reason, Christian perfection must involve an imitation of Jesus, and the role of the counsels is of especial importance here, for they "have the power to conform the Christian...more fully to that kind of virginal and poor life which Christ the Lord chose for himself and which his Virgin Mother embraced also" (*LG* 46). They define the life of Christ "who, virginal and poor, redeemed and sanctified men by obedience unto death on the cross" (*PC* 1). Thus the way of the counsels represents a clearer and more complete way of being conformed to Christ, the source of all holiness.

> "Our holy profession contains in embryo the whole of religious sanctity, and to achieve perfection in this sublime vocation there is no need to seek beyond this capital grace. A religious profession leads infallibly to sanctity." (Blessed Columba Marmion, OSB)

Sign of the heavenly kingdom

The consecrated life points to heaven, to an existence where God will be all in all. If the consecrated life looks back to paradise, it also looks forward to the future kingdom. Heaven is the perfection of love and reveals the limitless depth of the threefold gift of love that are the vows. In heaven there will be the perfection of chastity, for with body and soul all will live to God. There will be the perfection of poverty, for the saints hold all things in common in the sharing of all good things eternally. Obedience will reveal itself as the complete and ever-increasing readiness to be united to the will of God, and to recognise this will as the rule and fulfilment of one's own being and greater happiness.

Each of the counsels shows that we are made for God. However, this prophetic role in the Church is accomplished above all by means of consecrated chastity, which tradition has understood as "an especially expressive foretaste of the possession of Christ as the one bridegroom, as will occur in the fullness of the life to come."[19] As Jesus explained in the Gospels, in the world of the resurrection, people will "neither marry, nor are they given in marriage". The consecrated man or woman shows by their life that such a life has already begun. They point to the final condition of all men and women, one that is destined to last forever. "What we shall be," writes St Cyprian, addressing consecrated women, "you have already begun to be." The consecrated life "more fully manifests to all believers the presence of heavenly goods already possessed here below" (*LG* 44). The Vatican II document on religious life, *Perfectae Caritatis*, calls the life of the evangelical counsels "a clear symbol of the heavenly Kingdom".

The kingdom of heaven is something already and not yet. The kingdom has already come in Jesus, but in another sense it has not yet arrived. That is why we pray "Thy kingdom come". But since the kingdom has already come in Christ, it is now possible for some to be called by God to choose even now to live as people do in the final condition of the kingdom.

This perspective also explains why this special consecration of our chastity is not a sacrament. As a second baptism, the consecrated life expresses a certain death to the world, like martyrdom; as an expression of an undivided love for Christ, it points to the nuptial destiny of every person. Both these realities are eschatological, final states demanding no sacrament. Human marriage is a sacramental sign, a symbol of the divine reality of love between Christ and his Church. Those who profess consecrated chastity in search of an undivided love of Christ live out this reality here and now. Whereas the sacraments are a means, consecrated chastity is the final reality already with us.

By calling a person to live this life, God calls him or her to share in something of the perfection and grace of the other life. One is singled out by God and given a task in the Church to be a sign which presents visibly before the world that all are called to union with Christ.

"I am in Him, and He in me. As the Bishop was putting the ring on my finger, God pervaded my whole being, and since I cannot express that moment, I will be silent about it. My relationship with God, since perpetual vows, has been more intimate than it had ever been before. I sense that I love God and that He loves me. Having once tasted God, my soul could not live without Him. One hour spent at the foot of the altar in the greatest dryness of spirit is dearer to me than a hundred years of worldly pleasures. I prefer to be a lowly drudge in the convent than a queen in the world."

(St Faustina on her profession day)

Spousal character

For all Christ's faithful, consecrated men and women "recall that wonderful marriage made by God, which will be fully manifested in the future age, and in which the Church has Christ for her only spouse" (*PC* 12). *Lumen Gentium* says more simply that in consecrated life "Christ, joined to his Bride the Church by an indissoluble bond, is better represented" (*LG* 44).

The spouse of Christ is first of all the Church, as St Paul explains in the letter to the Ephesians. As St Augustine teaches, "A Bridegroom He has called Himself in the head, a Bride in the Body" (*Enarrationes in Psalmos*, 74). The Church is Bride insofar as she owes her existence to Christ as to her head. If consecrated chastity is the key or "door" to all the vows, it is because in consecrated chastity one sees clearly how the consecrated life is a way of being and representing the Church as Bride in a radical gift of self for love of our Lord Jesus Christ and in him of every member of the human family. Thus consecrated life is the sign of that union of the Son and humanity of which the Church is a sacrament - a union based on the Son's total gift of himself to humanity in the incarnation and redemption. It is spousal in character in order that it may manifest the exclusivity and personal nature of the love of the Son who "by his Incarnation... in a certain way united himself with each man" (*GS* 2).

The Church sees all consecrated life as the sign of the nuptial mystery of the Church as Bride, totally devoted to her Lord with an undivided heart, open and ready to receive her life and truth from him. In *Vita Consecrata*, St John Paul II teaches that at the very heart of the Church, as gift to the Church, the consecrated life manifests "the inner nature of the Christian calling, the striving of the whole Church as Bride towards union with her one Spouse" (*VC* 1). And at the very end, we read: "The Church can in no way renounce the consecrated life, for it eloquently expresses her inmost nature as 'Bride'" (*VC* 105).

Because it is spousal in character, the state of the counsels represents that total surrender to God in love which is the essence of sanctity and the very being of the Church: the Bride perfectly submitted to her spouse.[20] Hans Urs von Balthasar describes this well: "It is the primary function of one in the state of the counsels... to represent the Body, the Church-Bride... It is his task to assimilate the 'yes' of the whole Church to the 'yes' of Mary, whose model is her Son."[21]

> "From yesterday I belong entirely to our Lord. About seven o'clock I made my vows; about eleven o'clock a few locks of my hair were cut off in the church, then my head was shaved, leaving the monastic crown. And now I no longer belong to myself in any

way... I am in a state I have never experienced. It is a craving for meditation and silence, for lying at God's feet and looking at Him almost in silence. One feels, and would like to go on indefinitely feeling, that one belongs entirely to God, and that He is all our own. The 'Is it, then, nothing to belong all to God?' of St Teresa, furnishes the prayer."

(Blessed Charles de Foucauld, *Letter*, 3 February 1892)

Objective superiority

If profession of the evangelical counsels characterises the consecrated life, and if the counsels go "beyond the measure of the commandment", does this mean that the "consecrated life" is somehow superior to other callings in the Church? The constant tradition of the Church insists on the objective superiority of the consecrated life.[22]

"Christian tradition has always spoken of the objective superiority of the consecrated life." (*VC* 18)

"As a way of showing forth the Church's holiness, it is to be recognized that the consecrated life, which mirrors Christ's own way of life, has an objective superiority." (*VC* 32)

This teaching certainly does not mean that those who are called to consecrated life are in fact "superior" to or holier than other people. Holiness is ultimately measured by one's charity, not one's state in life. There is a distinction to be drawn between the *objective* value of a state of life and the *subjective* holiness of those who live it. An "objective superiority" has always been attributed to the consecrated life, on the grounds of its immediate reference to God and the goals of the Christian life, while at the same time acknowledging the human frailty of those living it.

The phrase "objective superiority" is *vitae consecratae praestantia* in Latin. Although *praestantia* implies a degree of comparison, and can mean superiority, it does not necessarily imply a direct comparison against something else. From the context, St John Paul II does not seem to intend that. There is no suggestion that a comparison is being made to the detriment of the unconsecrated life. Indeed, just before this paragraph he describes how the different states of life are not opposed, but are all manifestations of one or other dimension of the mystery of Christ. Moreover, the other states of life recall to consecrated persons the totality of the mystery of Christ and invite them to live fully their own adhesion to this mystery. The unity of the Christian life is displayed in these different vocations as so many rays from a single source of light which together make the face of Christ shine out.

A better translation, and that used in the German and French renderings of the text, might be "objective excellence". But however it is translated, it is clear that the Church wishes to insist that the consecrated life stands out in the Church. Why?

- It mirrors Christ's own way of life, "a way which may be called *divine*, for it was embraced by Him, God and man, as the expression of His relationship as the Only-Begotten Son with the Father and with the Holy Spirit" (*VC* 18).

- It is an especially rich manifestation of gospel values.

- It is a more complete expression of the Church's purpose: the sanctification of humanity. The religious life recalls the demand for holiness inherent in the Christian condition.

- It proclaims and anticipates the future age, when children of the resurrection will "neither marry nor be given in marriage but will be like the angels". The Church recognises that religious life as canonically defined is a sign of what the Church as a whole is called to be.

The objective excellence of the consecrated life does not reside in the personal merits of religious as individuals, let alone as a class, but rather in what gives religious life its meaning: the capacity of a human life to be in Christ a sacrament of the encounter with God. It becomes subjective when consecrated persons incarnate in their daily life the spirit of the beatitudes.

Sign and instrument of communion in the Church

Vatican II called the Church "the universal sacrament of salvation" (*LG* 48; *AG* 1), a sign and instrument of that communion with God to which all are called (*LG* 1). The Church as Bride is essentially a mystery of communion. Fraternal life, a life shared in love, seeks to reflect the depths and riches of this mystery.

When Christ instituted the state of consecrated life, he did so in virtue of individual calls, but at the same time he created around him a community. The life of communion begins with the fraternity, friendship and communion that Christ established with his disciples and which is prolonged in the first Christian community, the Church at Jerusalem described in the Acts of the Apostles.

Community life is one of the defining elements of the religious life. In Canon law we find this:

"The life of brothers or sisters proper to each institute, by which all members are united together like a special family in Christ, is to be determined in such a way that it becomes mutual support for all in fulfilling the vocation of each member. Moreover, by their communion as brothers or sisters, rooted in and built on love, the members are to be an example of universal reconciliation in Christ." (*CIC* 602)

The common life is an actualisation of that first Christian community, that life in which the members were "of one heart and one soul" (*Ac* 4:32). This fraternity expressed itself in a total sharing of material possessions. The material and spiritual fellowship of community life is an attitude, an environment that reflects the generosity of God towards us, the gift of God; ultimately Christian community springs from the life of the Trinity itself. This is reflected in Christ's prayer in John 17:21: "that all may be one, as you Father are in me and I in you". Christian community is the fruit of this prayer, fruit of the risen life of Christ. In this sense it is always a gift of God to man. It reflects, in time, the life of the Trinity itself.

St John Paul II in *Vita Consecrata* (21) brings together these two models of community life:

"Even fraternal life, whereby consecrated persons strive to live in Christ with 'one heart and one soul' (Acts 4:32) is put forward as an eloquent witness to the Trinity. It proclaims the Father who desires to make all humanity one family. It proclaims the Incarnate Son who gathers the redeemed into unity, pointing the way by his example, his prayer, his words, above all by his death which is the source of reconciliation for divided and scattered humanity. It proclaims the Holy Spirit as the principle of unity in the Church, wherein he raises up spiritual families and fraternal communities."

The vows express not only consecration to God but also dedication to community. By the practice of consecrated chastity the entire community professes that the love which motivates and directs them comes not from what is humanly pleasing, but from the action of the Holy Spirit within the hearts of each. Obedience is promised both to superiors and to one another; it is not only a surrender of one's own will but also an expression of following the common will. Poverty, as common ownership, sustains and expresses brotherhood in Christ. Poverty is both ascetical - the absence of possessions - and a sharing and giving of common possessions in Christ.

"It is certainly not beyond almighty God to grant instant perfection to everyone and bestow all the virtues on each of us, but his loving arrangement for us is that we should need one another... Each one's gift belongs to the community and each one shares in all the community offers." (St Aelred)

Loving with the Heart of the Redeemer

What are the distinctive elements of the mission of the consecrated life?

The apostolate of the vows

If the vows are a path to holiness, tools by which consecrated persons grow in sanctity, they also mobilise religious in the service of God for the extension of his kingdom and the salvation of all men. The vows purify and free the soul, but they also possess considerable power for the apostolate. Indeed one can speak of the apostolate of the vows, just as one speaks of the apostolate of prayer, the word, sacrifice and works. The observance of the vows is an apostolate of sanctity, for holiness is the greatest apostolate of all, shining forth and bearing fruit for the world. They help in the work of redemption since they cannot be practised without sacrifice. Through the vows, the consecrated life is a living preaching of the gospel.

Mission is not so much in the order of doing as in the order of being: conformity to Christ, keeping alive the way of life embraced by the Son of God. The consecrated person confesses Jesus Christ by his very way of life; he participates in and represents Christ before the world.

Consecration is already mission because it implies personal conversion. It points to the fact that the first mission consists in allowing oneself to be evangelised, purified. The world begins its return to the Father - the ultimate aim of every mission - beginning with the converted and transformed heart of the consecrated person. The whole history of consecrated life shows that the transformed heart, shaped by the vows, can sustain the most difficult and heroic undertakings for the world.

"Jesus told me: 'In convents too, there are souls that fill My Heart with joy. They bear My features; therefore the Heavenly Father looks upon them with special pleasure. They will be a marvel to Angels and men. Their number is very small. They are a defence for the world before the justice of the Heavenly Father and a means of obtaining mercy for the world. The love and sacrifice of these souls sustain the world in existence. The infidelity of a soul specially chosen by Me wounds My Heart most painfully. Such infidelities are swords which pierce My Heart.'" (St Faustina)

Community life

Fraternal life in community, as we have seen, is also a form of apostolate. By their fraternal love, consecrated persons show they are true disciples: "By this all will know that you are my disciples, if you have love for one another" (*Jn* 13:35). The mission of community life is not to do something, but to be reunited in community, to experience the presence of the Lord by the fact of this being together. As St Augustine expressed it in his rule: "Having a single heart and soul turned towards God: this is the reason for your coming together." Fraternal communion is already an apostolate and contributes directly to the work of evangelisation.

Wherever religious life is found, one of its main areas of witness is that of the reconciliation which Christ brings between brothers and sisters within the same Church. Thus the community, as a sign of this reconciliation which Christ brings about, is a sign of God's salvation, a sign of his grace and mercy; it is an anticipation, a prefiguration of the coming kingdom; it speaks to the world about the bonds that unite us all in Christ and with God.

Specific mission

The consecrated person is in mission both by virtue of his consecration and according to the purpose of his own institute. Both represent Christ, who is both the one consecrated to the Father and the one sent out into the world for the salvation of his brothers and sisters. The Lord Jesus is present not only through his way of being, but also in his way of acting, through the various religious institutes raised up by the Spirit throughout history, each with its own specific mission. Through the consecrated life, "the Church thus portrays Christ in contemplation on the mountain, in His proclamation of the kingdom of God to the multitudes, in His healing of the sick and maimed, in His work of converting sinners to a better life, in His solicitude for youth and His goodness to all men, always obedient to the will of the Father who sent Him" (*LG* 46).

The specific contribution of consecrated persons will be to witness to the love of Christ by prolonging his way of being and acting in the world, by becoming the heart of Christ, the hands of Christ, the mouth of Christ, "another humanity" of Christ in the world. The different forms of religious life are designed to perpetuate and to represent the various forms of our Lord's activity, whether in his life of prayer or of preaching, or his care for the sick and suffering.

Consecration is mission because it is an eloquent sign of divine love. Consecrated life shows that a life dedicated to God produces as a consequence devotion to one's neighbour in imitation of their beloved Lord who became a servant, laying down his life for others. It shows that in the work of salvation, everything springs from the self-giving love of Christ, received, lived, poured out. The form and foundation of the mission of the consecrated life is the cross.

The consecrated life is a manifestation of God's love in the world. The consecrated life is really a great love affair, the greatest there can be: a love for God and his Christ, a love for all men and women, a love ceaselessly renewed by the power of God's own love which comes to us in Christ.

"In the morning of September 8, I felt as though I were flooded with a river of peace, and it was in this peace which surpasses all understanding that I pronounced my Holy Vows... What graces I begged for on that day! I really felt I was the Queen and so I profited from my title by delivering captives, by obtaining favours from the King for His ungrateful subjects, finally, I wanted to deliver all the souls from purgatory and convert all sinners... I felt that time could not take away my happiness."

(St Thérèse of Lisieux on her profession day, 8 September 1890)

In *Vita Consecrata*, Pope St John Paul II presented the waste of the expensive perfume at Bethany as the symbol of the consecrated life:

"Many people today are puzzled and ask: What is the point of the consecrated life? The precious ointment poured out as an act of pure love, and thus transcending all 'utilitarian' considerations is a sign of unbounded generosity, as expressed in a life spent in loving and serving the Lord, in order to surrender oneself to his person and his Mystical Body. From such a life "poured out" without reserve there spreads a fragrance which fills the whole house." (*VC* 104)

Without the consecrated life, affirmed Pope Paul VI, charity would grow cold, the paradox of the gospel would be blunted, and the salt of faith would lose its savour. The Church and the world need the witness of the consecrated life; they need people capable of devoting themselves totally to God and others for the love of God. The consecrated life in its total and disinterested gift of the person to the Lord is a sign for others. The consecrated person's radical embracing of the Christian life is a reminder to others of what they are called to, namely, eternal life. It is a living invitation to others to follow Christ in their state of life. It is a reminder of the universal call to holiness that is union with God. That is why the Church holds on so firmly to the consecrated life, why she strives to do all she can to safeguard and develop it. And this radical gift of self is, paradoxically, not a loss but a gain. Consecrated life is a pearl of great price.

On the night of 26-27 March 1996, seven French Cistercian monks were kidnapped from their monastery in the Atlas Mountains in Algeria. They were found dead on 21 May 1996. In 2010, the director Xavier Beauvois turned the last year or so of their lives into the film Of Gods and Men. In one scene, Fr Luc, who is also a doctor, is asked by a young woman whether he has ever been in love: "Several times, yes. And then I encountered another love, even greater. And I answered that love. It's been a while now. Over 60 years."

Abbreviations

AG *Ad Gentes*, Decree on the Mission Activity of the Church, 1965.

CCC *Catechism of the Catholic Church* (2000)

GS *Gaudium et Spes*, Pastoral Constitution on the Church In the Modern World, 1965.

LG *Lumen Gentium*, Dogmatic Constitution on the Church, 1964.

PC *Perfectae Caritatis*, Decree on Renewal of Religious Life, 1965.

RD *Redemptionis Donum*, (Apostolic Exhortation to Religious Men and Women, Pope St John Paul II, 1984)

VC *Vita Consecrata*, On the Consecrated Life (Apostolic Exhortation of Pope John Paul II, 1996)

VS *Veritatis Splendor*, The Splendour of Truth: Regarding Certain Fundamental Questions of the Church's Moral Teaching (Encyclical of Pope John Paul II, 1993)

Endnotes

[1] *Essential Elements in the Church's Teaching on Religious Life as Applied to Institutes Dedicated to Works of the Apostolate*, III, I, 2.

[2] Though Vatican II did not use this term in connection with the consecrated life, recent popes do, e.g., Paul VI, *Evangelica testificatio* n. 11; John Paul II, Allocution to male religious in Sao Paulo, July 3, 1980.

[3] Commentary on Romans 10, 14, 7.

[4] *On Holy Virginity*, 15.

[5] *Summa Theologica*, 1-2, 108, 4.

[6] See *Treatise on the Love of God*, Bk. VIII, ch. 6-9

[7] Tradition has also sensed that they form a whole. For St Thomas (*Summa Theologica* 1-2, 108, 4), every particular counsel ultimately falls under the head of poverty, chastity or obedience, e.g. almsgiving goes back to poverty, temporary abstinence to chastity, forgiving enemies to self-renunciation in obedience. And, more importantly, these three principal counsels or vows are seen as embracing - in renunciation - the totality of an individual's existence: his external possessions, his body, his will.

[8] According to their Rule, Benedictines profess stability, conversion of life and obedience. It is only since the late 12th century, some 700 years after St Benedict, that it has been the universal practice for religious to make explicit vows of consecrated chastity, poverty and obedience. If the evangelical counsels have to be assumed by vow in religious profession, how is this done in Benedictine profession? There have been two answers given in the Benedictine tradition. One has seen chastity, poverty and obedience as implicitly included under conversion of life (*conversio morum*). The other has seen them as implicitly contained in all three vows or the profession itself.

[9] A Bull of Innocent IV (1247-1254) speaks of obedience, renunciation of private property and perpetual celibacy as the *substantialia* of any form of religious life. Such teaching is found, for example, in Vatican II's *Lumen Gentium* and *Perfectae Caritatis*, in John Paul II's *Redemptionis Donum* and *Vita Consecrata*, and in the *Catechism of the Catholic Church*.

[10] See, e.g., St Thomas Aquinas, *Summa Theologica* 1-2, 108, 4c; 2-2, 189, 4c; 184, 3, ad 1.

[11] *De perfectione vitae spiritualis*, c. 6; (*Summa Theologica* 1-2, 108, 4).

[12] For St Thomas, the three counsels are given us to remove the impediments arising from the things of this world. "Now the goods of this world...consist in three things, viz. in external wealth pertaining to the 'concupiscence of the eyes'; carnal pleasures pertaining to the 'concupiscence of the flesh'; and honours which pertain to the 'pride of life', according to *1 John* 2:16, and it is in renouncing these altogether, as far as possible, that the evangelical counsels consist. Moreover, every form of the religious life that professes the state of perfection is based on these three: since riches are renounced by poverty, carnal pleasures by perpetual chastity, and the pride of life by the bondage of obedience" (*Summa Theologica* 1-2, 108, 4).

[13] *De perfectione vitae spiritualis*, see 11; II-II q.186 a. 1; art. 7.

[14] *Summa Theologica* 2-2, 186, 8.

[15] The evolution of this terminology is significant. Both *LG* 6 and *PC* speak of religious life; *VC* uses the expression "consecrated life", indicating a more vivid awareness of the rich variety of forms of consecrated life. All religious are consecrated persons, but not all forms of deeper dedication to Christ and His Church are religious. Hermits, consecrated virgins and widows are truly consecrated, but are not bound to live in community. Societies of Apostolic Life (Oratorians, Paulist Fathers, Mill Hill Fathers, Daughters of Charity of St Vincent de Paul, etc.) are not religious in the full sense as they do not profess vows, but they do live in community. Only religious institutes, both contemplative and apostolic, possess both elements: the consecration through profession of vows and fraternal life in community.

72

[16] *Summa Theologica* II, 88, 6; 86, 6 ad 2.

[17] This teaching is summarised in *Essential Elements in the Church's Teaching on Religious Life*: "Consecration is the basis of religious life. By insisting on this, the Church places the first emphasis on the initiative of God and on the transforming relation to Him which religious life involves. Consecration is a divine action. God calls a person whom He sets apart for a particular dedication to Himself." (n. 5). John Paul II, *Redemptionis donum* n. 7; his speech to the American bishops, September 19, 1983, *L'Osservatore Romano* No. 216 (19-20 Sept 1983), p. 4.

[18] See e.g. St Thomas Aquinas, *Summa Theologica* 1-2, 108, 4c; 2-2, 189, 4c; 184, 3, ad 1.

[19] John Paul II, General Audience, 23 November 1994.

[20] This explains why the Magisterium excludes all attempts to redefine religious life in terms that would open it equally to people living in marriage, but has approved forms of the consecrated life, such as virginity lived in the world, where no explicit profession of poverty and obedience is involved (Can. 604).

[21] Hans Urs von Balthasar, *The Christian States of Life*, trans. by Sr. Mary Francis McCarthy (San Francisco: Ignatius Press, 1983), p. 278.

[22] See The Holy Council of Trent session 24, canon 10; Pope Pius XII, *Sacra Virginitas* issued during the Marian Year of 1954; *Optatam Totius* (no. 10) on the training of priests.